# believe
# and
# achieve.

Author: Sasha Morton
Design: Bag of Badgers Ltd.

ISBN: 978-1-916992-31-3

Printed in China

10 9 8 7 6 5 4 3 2 1

Welcome to **Believe and Achieve** – a collection of **modern and relatable quotes** that will **inspire you to aim for new heights of success and fulfilment**. Whatever goals you set yourself, there will be something in these pages to encourage you to follow your dreams. Make yourself comfortable and take on board these words of encouragement, experience and wit – then go out there and take on the world!

**Enjoy!**

We don't even know how strong we are until we are forced to bring that hidden strength forward. In times of tragedy, of war, of necessity, people do amazing things. The human capacity for survival and renewal is awesome.

Isabel Allende

Do something **wonderful**.
People may
**IMITATE**
it.

Albert Schweitzer

You've got to invest in the world, you've got to read, you've got to go to art galleries, you've got to find out the names of plants. You've got to start to love the world and know about the whole genius of the human race. We're amazing people.

Vivienne Westwood

Creativity
takes
courage.

Henri Matisse

**Continuous improvement is better than delayed perfection.**

Mark Twain

It's the
possibility of having
a dream come true
that makes life
interesting.

Paulo Coelho

You have to
    trust in something –
**your gut**,
    **destiny**,
        **life**,
            **karma**,
                **whatever**.
**This approach has
never let me down,
and it has made all
the difference in my life.**

Steve Jobs

In
**The Book
of Life,**
the answers
aren't in
the back.

Charles M Schulz

I believe in
**being strong**
when everything
seems to be
going wrong.

Audrey Hepburn

No matter what
people tell you,
**words and ideas**
**<u>can</u>**
**change the**
**world**.

Robin Williams

**Be the designer of your own destiny.**

Oscar de la Renta

**You never know how strong you are, until being strong is your only choice.**

Bob Marley

The whole point
of being alive
is to evolve into
the complete
person you were
intended to be.

Oprah Winfrey

**DON'T** underestimate the importance of happiness. **As long as you're happy**, who cares what you do?

John Lennon

# Be persistent and never give up hope.

George Lucas

You can't just be talented:
You have to be terribly smart
and energetic and ruthless. You
also have to become necessary
to people, by working hard and
well and bringing more than
your bones and your skin to
the project. Don't just show up.
Transform the work, yourself,
and everybody around you.
Be needed. Be interesting. Be
something no one else can be
– and consistently.

Katherine Hepburn

Success isn't always about greatness. It's about consistency. Consistent hard work leads to success. **GREATNESS WILL COME.**

Dwayne 'The Rock' Johnson

I love what I do. I take great pride in what I do. And I can't do something halfway, three-quarters, nine-tenths. **If I'm going to do something, I go all the way.**

Tom Cruise

**Life is ten percent what you make it, and ninety percent how you take it.**

Irving Berlin

My best life lessons and education didn't come from a classroom – they've come from the wild. How you act in the big moments, the ones that challenge you, scare you, tempt you, and force you to make the right decisions, is what defines you.

Bear Grylls

Ambition is a funny thing:
it creeps in when you least
expect it and keeps you
moving, even when you
think you want to stay put.

Lena Dunham

The people who put
you down don't have to
stop you from chasing
your dreams. Stand up,
and prove them wrong.

Selena Gomez

I'm such a profound believer that timing is everything; I would tattoo that on my arm.

Drew Barrymore

My new one [tattoo] says,

'**Never a failure,
always a lesson**'

and is kind of my mantra
to life, just a reminder.
My life is just a crazy
rollercoaster every day
and whenever I read that
it just reassures me.

Rihanna

Never doubt that you are
**VALUABLE**
**AND**
**POWERFUL**
and deserving of every
chance in the world to
**PURSUE**
**YOUR**
**DREAMS.**

Hillary Clinton

I'm not going to continue knocking that old door that doesn't open for me.

I'm going to create my own door and walk through that.

Ava DuVernay

I've missed more than 9,000 shots in my career.

I've lost almost 300 games.

26 times, I've been trusted to take the game winning shot and missed.

I've failed over and over and over again in my life.

And that is why I succeed.

Michael Jordan

Success
is about
**falling nine times**
and
**getting up ten.**

Jon Bon Jovi

**Be strong,
be fearless,
be beautiful.
And believe**
that anything is
possible when you
have the right people
there to support you.

Misty Copeland

You become
what you
believe, **not**
what you
think or what
you want.

Oprah Winfrey

I would say to always follow your dream. And dream big because my whole career, including any of the things that I've accomplished, I never thought in a million years that I would be here. So it just proves that once you believe in yourself, and you put your mind to something, you can do it.

Simone Biles

A positive
attitude can
really make
**dreams**
**come**
**true –**
**IT DID FOR ME.**

David Bailey

# Attitude is a little thing that makes a big difference.

Winston Churchill

Whatever your situation might be, set your mind to whatever you want to do and put a good attitude in it, and I believe that you can succeed. You are not going to get anywhere just sitting on your butt and moping around.

Bethany Hamilton

Some people say
**I have attitude** –
maybe I do ...
but I think you have to.

You have to believe
in yourself when
no one else does –
that **makes you a
winner** right there.

Serena Williams

I still say,
'SHOOT FOR
THE MOON;
YOU MIGHT
GET THERE.'

Buzz Aldrin

If you are lucky enough
to find something
that you love,

and you have
a shot at being
good at it,

**DON'T STOP,**

don't put it down.

Taylor Swift

Find something you're passionate about and keep tremendously interested in it.

Julia Child

However difficult
life may seem,
there is
**always something**
you can do and
succeed at.

Stephen Hawking

Inside every
lump of coal
there is a

diamond
waiting to
get out.

Terry Pratchett

The only place where success comes before work is in the dictionary.

Vidal Sassoon

One must
work and
dare if one
really wants
to live.

Vincent Van Gogh

Trust yourself.
Create the kind of
self that you will
be happy to live
with all your life.

Golda Meir

If I had to live
my life again,
I'd make the
same mistakes,
only sooner.

Tallulah Bankhead

As you navigate through
the rest of your life,
**be open to collaboration**.
Other people and
other people's ideas are
**often better than your own**.

Amy Poehler

Just say YES
and you'll
figure it out
afterwards.

Tina Fey

There are a lot of comedians that were bullied and picked on, and that's why they became comedians. Survival of the fittest.

Tiffany Haddish

I believe that if life gives you lemons, you should make lemonade … and try to find somebody whose life has given them vodka, and have a party.

Ron White

The most important thing is to try and inspire people so that they can be great in whatever they want to do.

Kobe Bryant

I know
my body.
I know
my mind.
I know
what I can do.

Wim Hof

No matter what you're going through, there's a light at the end of the tunnel and it may seem hard to get to it but you can do it and just keep working towards it and you'll find the positive side of things.

Demi Lovato

If you think you can do better, then do better.

Don't compete with anyone; just yourself.

Bob Fosse

It's a good thing to imagine yourself doing something you think you can't. I do that every day because, basically, if I had it my way, I'd just stay home and think about what I'm having for supper.

Meryl Streep

The mind is the limit.

As long as the mind can envision the fact that you can do something, **you can do it,** as long as you really believe 100 percent.

Arnold Schwarzenegger

If you organize your life around your passion, you can turn your passion into your story and then turn your story into something bigger — something that matters.

Blake Mycoskie,
founder of TOMS Shoes

Focus more
on your desire
than on your doubt,
and the dream will
take care of itself.

Mark Twain

Know your
**power**,
believe in
**yourself**,
and don't anyone
**dim your light.**

Leigh-Anne Pinnock

Sometimes
it's the journey
that teaches
you a lot
about your
destination.

Drake

I don't want
to be remembered
as the girl who
**WAS SHOT**.

I want to
be remembered
as the girl
**WHO STOOD UP**.

Malala Yousafzai

Change happens by **listening**, and then starting a **dialogue** with the people you don't believe are doing something right.

Jane Goodall

I am
**not designed**
to come
second or third.
I am
designed to
**WIN.**

Ayrton Senna

Every twist and turn in your life is an opportunity to learn something new about **yourself**, **your interests**, **your talents**, and how to set and then achieve **goals**.

Jameela Jamil

There is no passion
to be found playing
small – in settling
for a life that is less
than the one you
are capable of living.

Nelson Mandela

If everyone
is moving
forward together,
then success
takes care
of itself.

Henry Ford

With drive and
a bit of talent,
you can
move mountains.

I know.
I'VE DONE IT.

Dwayne 'The Rock' Johnson

Don't
count the days,
make the days
COUNT.

Muhammad Ali

# SUCCESS IS NO ACCIDENT.

It is hard work, perseverance, learning, studying, sacrifice and most of all, love of what you are learning to do.

Pelé

If you
do not believe
you can do it,
then you have
no chance at all.

Arsène Wenger

The more you
are positive and say,
'I want to have a good life,'
the more you build that
reality for yourself by
creating the life that
you want.

Chris Pine

My father taught me
not to overthink things,
that nothing will ever
**be perfect**,
so just keep moving
**and do your best.**

Scott Eastwood

If you want to be
the best,
you have to do
things that other
people aren't
willing to do.

Michael Phelps

Everything I dared dream of has come to fruition. Which is not to say that I don't grumble with the best of them, but the wobbles have been way outweighed by the wonders.

Richard E Grant

Ultimately, leadership is not about **glorious crowning acts.** It's about keeping your team **focused** on a goal and **motivated** to do their best to achieve it, especially when the stakes are high and the consequences really matter. It is about laying the groundwork for others' success, and then standing back and **letting them shine.**

Chris Hadfield

There is
**ONLY ONE CORNER**
**OF THE UNIVERSE**
you can be certain
of improving, and
that's your
**OWN SELF.**

Aldous Huxley

I'm on the path
to being someone
    I'm equally terrified by
    and obsessed with.
    My true self.

Troye Sivan

If you don't keep paddling,
you're never going to
catch a wave.
**So I just keep paddling**.

Kylie Minogue

I would love to go back in time and tell my younger self,

'Michelle, these middle and high school years are just a tiny blip in your life, and all the slights and embarrassments and heartaches, all those times you got that one question wrong on that test – **none of that is important in the scheme of things**'.

Michelle Obama

When
we love
ourselves,
we make
good choices.

Jennifer Lopez

Many people worry so much about managing their careers, but rarely spend half that much energy managing their LIVES.

I want to make my life, not just my job, the best it can be. The rest will work itself out.

Reese Witherspoon

There's **nothing wrong** with being driven. And there's **nothing wrong** with putting yourself first to **reach your goals**.

Shonda Rhimes

Every morning I want to wake up and be excited about what I'm going to do.

I want it to be honest and fulfilling for me personally, and then maybe it can be fulfilling for the rest of the world, too.

Jacob Elordi

I foresee a world which is
**more creative,**
**more open,**
**more loving,**
**more ecologically friendly,**
**more honest about its**
**history and progress,**
and I think a lot of those
contributions will be
**made by young people.**

Amanda Gorman

My mother told me
two things constantly.
One was to
**be a lady**
and the other was to
**be independent**.

Ruth Bader Ginsburg

Don't look too far into the future, just look at tomorrow. One day at a time. Can you win tomorrow? Can you make progress? The answer is **yes**, you have a choice and tomorrow you're going to win.

Joe Wicks

I've learned that if I only put my mind to one thing that I can get tunnel vision. Then I may not be as open to other opportunities because I'm so focused on one thing. I think what's worked better for me personally is I have three goals every day:

**be nice,**
**work hard,**
**and make friends.**

Gigi Hadid

Like what
you do,
and then
you will do
your best.

Katherine Johnson

You can have
all the tools
in the world,

but

if you don't genuinely
believe in yourself,
it's useless.

Ken Jeong

When you have **balance in your life**, work becomes an entirely different experience. There is **a passion** that moves you to a whole new level of **fulfilment and gratitude**, and that's when you can do your best …
**for yourself and for others**.

Cara Delevingne

Quite simply,
my friends
inspire me
to strive.

Dan Levy

Do the best you can in every task, **no matter how unimportant it may seem at the time.** No one learns more about a problem than the person at the bottom.

Sandra Day O'Connor

# BE BOLD.

Be brave enough to be your true self.

Queen Latifah

I want to make sure that that future that we're creating is one that is the best it can be for people around the world, and also one that includes the full range of our talent and our skills.

Mae Jemison

People are
going to
judge you
anyway,
so you might
as well
**do what
you want.**

Taylor Swift

Every single thing
that I was told that
I COULDN'T DO
without a label – get in
the charts, get on to the
Radio 1 playlist –
I'VE DONE.

Stormzy

As long as you have discipline, you can be a success. Discipline is what makes you do everything you need to do.

Anthony Joshua

I hated every minute of training, but I said, 'Don't quit. Suffer now and live the rest of your life as a champion.'

Muhammad Ali

I wasn't born
ambitious,
but I am now.

Joe Wicks

I think the only way to achieve something that's classic is to be in the moment. You don't sit around and think,

'Oh, I hope this is remembered forever!'

You just have to be honest, and I think that requires being in the moment.

Justin Timberlake

Don't sit there
and **complain**.

Rub your
hands together
and **figure out**
what to do.

Michaela Coel

Thinking isn't always the answer. Sometimes the best thing to do is listen to everything **your heart, body and soul** are trying to tell you.

Claire Foy

**I'm self-made.** I always wanted to make myself a better person, because I was not educated. But that was my dream – **to have class.**

Tina Turner

Believe in love.
Believe in magic.
Hell, believe in Santa Claus.
Believe in others.
Believe in yourself.
Believe in your dreams.

**IF YOU DON'T,
WHO WILL?**

Jon Bon Jovi

We're here
for a reason.
I believe that reason is
to throw little torches
out **to lead people
through the dark**.

Whoopi Goldberg

You need to go where you
are loved – because that's
precisely the place where
your dreams and goals
will be nurtured. **People
who see the best in you,
bring out the best in you**.

Lupita Nyong'o

# DREAM AS IF YOU'LL LIVE FOREVER.
# LIVE AS IF YOU'LL DIE TODAY.

James Dean

If you know who you
are, and what you
can carry off, and
what you're going to
be comfortable with,
you do it.
Go for it.
Don't be afraid.

Iris Apfel

I started posting covers online and having this crazy determination about what I wanted to do and just went for it. I was like,

'Okay, no one else can create my future for me, and no one can get what I want for me, so I have to go out and get it myself.'

Dua Lipa

By using my career as the wind in the sails of my adventures, I could see so many things and so many people that I might have missed had my career gone a different direction.

Robert Plant

Whenever I feel bad, I use that feeling to motivate me to work harder. I only allow myself one day to feel sorry for myself. When I'm not feeling my best, I ask myself,

'What are you gonna do about it?'

I use the negativity to fuel the transformation into a better me.

Beyoncé

People respond well to those who are sure of what they want.

Anna Wintour

Failure is simply the non-presence of success.

But a fiasco is a DISASTER OF MYTHIC PROPORTIONS.

Orlando Bloom

My mother wanted us to understand that the tragedies of your life one day have the potential to be comic stories the next.

Nora Ephron

MY MOTHER
WAS RIGHT:
When you've
got nothing left,
all you can do is
get into silk underwear
and start reading Proust.

Jane Birkin

I like the night.
I have
clearer ideas
in the dark.

Serge Gainsbourg

I actually began my career by convincing my parents to let me be an actress when I was 12 with a PowerPoint presentation describing acting and my goals.

Sydney Sweeney

**IN LIFE YOU CAN'T LIE TO YOURSELF** – you have to look in the mirror and feel good about your choices … Listen to your gut and your instincts.

Nicola Coughlan

I have a strong sense of myself. That gives me a sense of security, you know? If I define myself by things that are always changing, like the public's opinion, or what I'm wearing, or what job I'm doing, there's **no stability in** that.

Blake Lively

You can have anything you want in life, if you dress for it.

Edith Head

I believe that people should take pride in what they do, even if it is scorned or misunderstood by the public at large.

Tony Hawk

I could give you a million reasons why you don't need to cater to anything or anyone to succeed.

**Be you, and be relentlessly you.** That's the stuff of **CHAMPIONS.**

Lady Gaga

Dreams are lovely,
but they are just dreams.

Fleeting, ephemeral, pretty.
But dreams do not come
true just because you dream
them. It's hard work that
makes things happen.

It's hard work that
creates change.

Shonda Rhimes

What would happen if we encouraged all women to be a little more ambitious?

**I THINK THE WORLD WOULD CHANGE.**

Reese Witherspoon

**I wouldn't say anything is impossible. I think that everything is possible** as long as you put your mind to it and put the work and time into it.

Michael Phelps

I love biting off more than I can chew and figuring it out.

Jordan Peele

**Success is most often achieved by those who don't know that failure is inevitable.**

Coco Chanel

It takes a certain grace, strength, intelligence, fearlessness, and the nerve to never take no for an answer.

Rihanna

I felt I had to do things, to be intelligent and develop a personality in order to be seen as attractive.

By the time I realized maybe I wasn't plain and might even possibly be pretty, I had already trained myself to be a little more interesting and informed.

Diane Von Furstenberg

Don't compromise yourself.

You are all you've got.

There is no yesterday,
no tomorrow,
it's all the same day.

Janis Joplin

The most
effective way
to do it,
is to do it.

Amelia Earhart

I have learned over
the years that

when one's mind
is made up, this
diminishes fear;

knowing what must be
done does away with fear.

Rosa Parks

If your actions create
a legacy that inspires
others to
  dream more,
    learn more,
      do more and
        become more,
then, you are an
EXCELLENT LEADER.

Dolly Parton

Understand
that one day
you will have
the power to
make a difference,
so
USE IT WELL.

Mindy Kaling

Don't be afraid of your ambition, of your dreams, or even your anger.

**Those are powerful forces.**

But harness them to make a difference in the world.

Hillary Clinton

You and
  you alone
are the only person
who can
  live the life
    that writes the story
that you were
    meant to tell.

Kerry Washington

Say
YES,
and
create
your
own
destiny.

Maya Rudolph

Dreams
are
extremely
important.

You can't do
it unless you
imagine it.

George Lucas

If you don't have a
Valentine, hang out
with your girlfriends,
don't go looking
for someone.
When it's right,
**they'll come to you**.

Carmen Electra

Every woman in her
late 20s goes through
a period where she
just doesn't believe
love is out there
anymore, but it is.

And I think the
minute you stop
looking for it is when
it comes for you.

Kristen Bell

If you're presenting yourself with **CONFIDENCE,**

you can pull off pretty much **ANYTHING.**

Katy Perry

Everything works out,
it's **okay**,
whatever's bothering
you in the moment
**will probably pass,**
you'll get through it.

Elizabeth Moss

My mama always
used to tell me:

'If you can't find
somethin' to live
for, you best find
somethin' to die for.'

Tupac Shakur

I SEE MYSELF AS THE
BEST FOOTBALLER
IN THE WORLD.

If you don't believe you
are the best, then you
will never achieve all that
you are capable of.

Cristiano Ronaldo

If you feel like there's something out there that you're supposed to be doing, if you have a passion for it, then stop wishing and **JUST DO IT**.

Wanda Sykes

I don't think we are going to become extinct. We're very clever and extremely resourceful – and we will find ways of preserving ourselves, of that, I'm sure. But whether our lives will be as rich as they are now, is another question.

Sir David Attenborough

What I find really
interesting is to try and
mix it up, to push myself
and try different things.
I don't want to stay in
my comfort zone.
I want to take risks and
keep myself scared.

Michael Fassbender

I think we all get into situations where we don't know how to proceed, and those are really the scariest moments that we have, but that's also what makes us 'grow up' and learn a lot about each other.

John Krasinski

Being polite and grateful will make people more inclined to help you. And if people are willing to help you, you may accidentally get something you want.

Jason Sudeikis

Nothing in life
is to be feared,
it is only to be
understood.

Now is the time
to understand
more, so that we
may fear less.

Marie Curie

# TRUST
# THE
# PROCESS.

Tony Wroten

As a driver, you've always got to believe in your heart that you've got what it takes to win it. You've always got to believe in yourself. You've always got to arrive on the day and believe it can happen. **You've always got to believe in the positives.**

Lewis Hamilton

# Try and fail, but <u>never</u> fail to try.

Jared Leto

Making words rhyme for a living is one of the great joys of my life … That's a superpower I've been very conscious of developing. I started at the same level as everybody else, and then I just listened to more music and talked to myself until it was an actual superpower I could pull out on special occasions.

Lin–Manuel Miranda

**If you have the opportunity to play this game called life, you have to appreciate every moment.**

Kanye West

I had an extraordinary belief in myself. For years people told me to give it up and even though I was poverty-stricken, I never thought I should give it up.

Michael Caine

He
who
has
the
**GOLD**
makes
the
rules.

Tyler Perry

If I was going to be successful, I had to be successful with myself.

I couldn't be successful doing what other people were doing … The worst thing to be is as successful as someone else.

That's a very difficult thing to upkeep and **very tiring**.

Jay–Z

Strength does not come from winning. Your struggles develop your strengths.

When you go through hardships and decide not to surrender, that is strength.

Arnold Schwarzenegger

# Success is a journey, not a destination.

Elton John

I don't say:
  'can't **do that**,
  **won't do that**'.
I've never thought in that way about work. The genuine truth, and I do think about this a lot, is that I'm one of the least competitive people you'll ever meet. Except with myself.

Daniel Craig

**Life comes with many challenges. The ones that should not scare us are the ones we can take on and take control of.**

Angelina Jolie

Your regrets
aren't what
**you did,**
but what
you **didn't do.**
So take
every opportunity.

Cameron Diaz

'**MAY THE FORCE BE WITH YOU**' is charming but it's not important.

What's important is that you **become the Force** — for yourself and perhaps for other people.

Harrison Ford

# Action is the foundational key to all success.

Pablo Picasso

My teacher said to me,
'If you're going to fail,
fail gloriously.'
I've never forgotten it.
You **learn a lot from your
mistakes**. You have to take
risks and make mistakes.
It's terrifying, but it's the
only way you will learn
and improve.

Cate Blanchett

I've learned it's important not to limit yourself.

You can do whatever you really love to do, no matter what it is.

Ryan Gosling

# Failures are infinitely more instructive than successes.

George Clooney

You can't knock on opportunity's door and not be ready.

Bruno Mars

The simple act of paying attention can take you a long way.

Keanu Reeves

Don't listen to what anybody says **except** the people who encourage you.

If it's what you want to do and it's within yourself, then keep going and try to do it for the rest of your life.

Jake Gyllenhaal

I don't want the **fear of failure** to stop me from doing what **I really care about.**

Emma Watson

The greatest danger
for most of us is not
that our aim is too
high and we miss it,

but that it is too low
and we reach it.

Michelangelo

You are never too
old to set another
goal or dream
another dream.

C S Lewis

Life is either
a daring
adventure, or
nothing at all.

Helen Keller

Mountains are only
a problem when
they are bigger
than your spirit.

Unknown

**If you aim higher than you expect, you could reach higher than you dreamed.**

Richard Branson

I'm continually trying to make choices that put me against my own comfort zone. As long as you're uncomfortable, it means you're growing.

Ashton Kutcher

If you put out
    150 percent,
then you can always expect
    100 percent back.
That's what I was
always told as a kid, and
it's worked for me so far!

Justin Timberlake

Don't become something just because someone else wants you to – or because it's easy. YOU WON'T BE HAPPY.

Kristen Wiig

**IGNORE THE NAYSAYERS.** Really the only option is, head down and focus on the job.

Chris Pine

I believe there's an **inner power** that makes winners or losers. And the winners are the ones who really **listen to the truth of** their hearts.

Sylvester Stallone

You have to wake up
every day and say,

'There's no reason
today can't be the
best day of my life'.

Blake Lively

It's never too late –
never too late to
start over,
never too late to
be happy.

Jane Fonda

I think once we let our ego go, [we] just get over the fact that everybody's not going to like us – and that's OK! Because there will be people who do dig it. And even if they don't, do you? You get one life. Who cares what everyone else thinks?

Kelly Clarkson

It's amazing what you can get if you quietly, clearly, and authoritatively **demand it**.

Meryl Streep

# If you risk nothing, then you risk everything.

Geena Davis

Work hard
in silence,
let success be
your noise.

Unknown

Just don't give up
trying to do what
you really want
to do.

Where there
is **love and
inspiration**,
I don't think you
can go wrong.

Ella Fitzgerald

I always told myself
never to have a plan B –
I feel like that's also one of
the reasons I'm doing what
I'm doing now, because
I just never really rested
until I got here.

Dua Lipa

# THROW CAUTION TO THE WIND AND JUST DO IT.

Carrie Underwood